Improving Literacy with ICT

A companion website to accompany this book is available online at:
http://education.millum.continuumbooks.com

Please type in the URL above and receive your unique password for access to the book's online resources.

If you experience any problems accessing the resources, please contact Continuum at:
info@continuumbooks.com

Also available from Continuum

100 Ideas for Teaching Literacy, Fred Sedgwick
Getting the Buggers Excited About ICT, Karen Anderson
Primary Schools and ICT, Neil Selwyn, Sue Cranmer and John Potter
Teaching English Using ICT, Tom Rank, Chris Warren and Trevor Millum

Improving Literacy with ICT

Ideas and Resources for Teaching Ages 7–12

Trevor Millum

continuum

Continuum International Publishing Group

The Tower Building	80 Maiden Lane
11 York Road	Suite 704
London	New York
SE1 7NX	NY 10038

www.continuumbooks.com

British Library Cataloguing-in-Publication Data
A catalogue record for this book is available from the British Library.

ISBN: 978-1-4411-9239-4 (paperback)

Library of Congress Cataloging-in-Publication Data
A catalog record for this book is available from the Library of Congress.

Typeset by Ben Cracknell Studios
Printed and bound in India

Contents

Acknowledgements

I'd like to thank my friends and colleagues at NATE for support and inspiration throughout my adventures in English over the last 35 years. Thanks also to Resource Education and especially to Peter Cave, the source of many great ideas and several mad ones.

Foreword

There can be no doubt that 21st-century children are immersed in technologies that were only a glimmer of a thought in the mind of an IT expert at the dawn of the new century. The prime use of mobile phones – which are now a must-have possession of the youngest primary-age child – is no longer just for talking. Their capacity for taking still and moving pictures and the accessibility of computer games, MP3 players and texting facilities mean that huge numbers of children are carrying in their pockets a device that magically transports them to other worlds. Of course, they still use the computer at home. They send emails and electronic greetings cards to family and friends, look at holiday photographs and play yet more games. Sometimes – if their school is able to use the facility – they have access to a Learning Platform or other safe e-space to email friends, download homework and use school-based software. It would seem that the information and communication world is a child's oyster.

However, in the middle of all this innovation, English language in all its forms remains central to this communication revolution, and literature is still a core feature of our cultural life. Children read and write at least as much as they have ever done. They read and write texts, emails and school blogs as well as using the 'old' paper and pencil technologies. They still read, maybe as much on an electronic device as from a book, but they have a love of stories – old and new – which are adapted for games, cartoon and film, but which may begin their life in the printed word to which children still return. They are moved and entertained by poetry and its power to reflect emotions and they are able to follow their own interests and research online and in the library. All of this, as James Britton reminded us over 30 years ago, 'floats on a sea of talk' and collaboration. It is a heady and complex mix of individually acquired accomplishments.

Where then does the primary classroom sit in all this? How can teachers make the best use of the technology that is available to them and their pupils? How should we currently approach the teaching of English? How might we motivate children, foster their interest in language and literature while encouraging them to learn both the language and ICT skills that they need for life?

In this book, Trevor Millum aims to help primary teachers answer some of these questions for themselves. He is committed to giving us very practical ideas that use ICT as a tool to help children to become more accomplished readers and writers across the curriculum – and in all of them the computer is essential. They are examples of what it means to integrate ICT within the curriculum. He does not expect us to be technical whizz kids. He is realistic about the practicalities of classroom equipment, but he does offer us some fresh ways of developing literacy using what we have. It isn't a book of worksheets – it is a book of ideas. Enjoy where it might take you and be fearless!

An accomplished poet, writer and teacher, Trevor understands the importance of keeping children engaged and motivated. He knows they need help in acquiring the technical skills of writing. He knows how much they enjoy playing with words and ideas and making links between things they have learned. He also knows that children are not afraid of the technology and that they will enjoy making it work for them.

As Trevor so rightly reminds us, the C in ICT is for Communication. I am sure that your pupils' talking, reading and writing, and ICT skills will grow as you build on the ideas in *Improving Literacy with ICT*.

Barbara Conridge
Education Consultant
Chair Primary Committee, National Association for the Teaching of English (NATE)

Introduction

Improving Literacy with ICT is not a book for 'techies'; it is a book for those who love language and literature, enjoy playing with words and want their pupils to be similarly engaged and motivated. The writer's background is that of a teacher and a children's author, not an ICT expert. Long ago, though, he realized the exciting possibilities that technology could offer teachers when used creatively and when, crucially, the focus remained on English rather than on the ICT.

Improving Literacy with ICT is intended as a source book of ideas, not a collection of lesson plans. It comprises a series of activities within the following chapters:

Frameworks

Transformations

Investigations and demonstrations

Communication

Pictures and sound

Presentations

Given that this is primarily a book of ideas, you are encouraged to adapt them, share them and pass them on. Those, after all, are some of the things that ICT allows us to do easily.

In the classroom

Many of the approaches described in this book will be applicable to a wide range of cross-curricular situations. To take an obvious example, Writing to Persuade or Inform in Chapter 1 is clearly relevant to work in history, science, RE and PSHE. A table is provided to suggest where an activity may be particularly relevant in another subject area (see page xiii).

Many activities lend themselves to pupils working in pairs and small groups. ICT can encourage discussion and group decision-making. Some activities make this an explicit part of the work; even where it is not, teachers should signal to pupils that on-task talk is a positive thing and that verbalizing thought is a good way of testing hypotheses.

Within each chapter there is a selection of activities. Most activities can be adapted to suit pupils of widely different ages and abilities. The table on page xiii suggests appropriate ages for different kinds of work. This must be taken as a very general guideline. Pupils vary enormously in their abilities, and young pupils even more so. Often, changing the text or the topic you are using will be enough to adapt work for a different audience. You, as the teacher, will be the best judge of the suitability of any particular activity.

Most activities will be followed by Development and Differentiation sections. These contain ideas which help you to do just that: build on what you have already done and take the activities further – or in a new direction and/or to adapt the activities to suit differing abilities.

Software and hardware

All of the activities can be carried out using commonly available software applications. Given that Word and PowerPoint are so widely known and available, these may be referred to in order to make explanations clear or to give examples. This does not imply any endorsement or that these programs are superior to others.

This book is based on the understanding that schools will not have a computer readily available for every child. Many activities can be carried out in groups or pairs and others can be carried out 'in relay'. Still others are activities to be used by the teacher in conjunction with a data projector.

Classroom organization

While the arrangement of classroom fittings is beyond the control of most teachers, it is worth thinking about improvements and making sure your voice is heard next time decisions of this kind are taken. In far too many classrooms, the computer connected to the projector is squashed into a small space facing a wall. How much better for the teacher to be able to face her class while using keyboard or mouse! Although pupil access to an interactive whiteboard has usually been considered, other options, such as wireless keyboards or mice, rarely have. These latter allow pupil interaction with a minimum of classroom movement and disruption.

Projectors and whiteboards

A projector to show a computer image on a screen or wall is a great help in any classroom. You do not need an interactive whiteboard to do this. Interactive whiteboards are a useful additional resource but not essential in order to demonstrate and involve pupils in many key language activities.

Worksheets

Some activities are accompanied by pupil worksheets which can be found at the back of the book as photocopiable pages. They are also included as files on the accompanying website, and may be adapted to suit your pupils' needs.

Files

Many activities use text extracts which are usually included as hard copy. These are also available on the accompanying website and may be adapted for your own use. Updates may be made available on the website as appropriate. If you have trouble accessing any of the files, open your word processor first, then go to Open or Import File and access the file from within the application.

Having access to the files in electronic form means that you will be able to alter them to suit your particular requirements.

The future

Given the nature of technology, some of the terminology in this book may well have changed by the time you read it! New possibilities will have opened up and new gadgets and gizmos will have appeared on the market. This book tries as far as possible to be future-proof in that the underlying principles should remain sound and the ideas and activities suggested will still be relevant even if the hardware or software used have changed.

Whenever you see this icon, you can visit the companion website (http://education.millum. continuumbooks.com) to find downloadable versions of texts, plus many more accompanying resources to use in your lessons.

Some cross-curricular links

Chapter	Activity	Other curriculum areas	Recommended age
Chapter 1	Narrative or autobiographical writing using starter texts		7+
	Writing to persuade or inform	History Geography RE PSHE	8+
	Poetry patterns		All ages
	Using PowerPoint to present an argument	History Geography RE PSHE	8+
Chapter 2	Sequencing	Science History Geography Modern Languages	7+
	Different audiences, different purposes	History	7+
	Just like fridge magnets	Modern Languages	6+
	Plays and dialogue		8+
	Making Improvements	All subjects	7+
Chapter 3	Investigating text types	History Geography RE Science PSHE	9+
	Investigating word classes		9+
	Using codes to investigate words and contexts	Modern Languages	9+
	Peeking into texts	History Geography RE Science PSHE Modern Languages	All ages
	Sentence building		6+
	Moving and making	Specialist words in, for example, Science, Geography	All ages
	Investigating poetry features		9+
Chapter 4	Publishing		All ages
	Researching	All subjects, including PE, Art and Music	7+
	Exchanging		7+
Chapter 5	Film	All subjects, including PE, Art and Music	6+
	Animation	Design/Technology plus all subjects, including PE, Art and Music	6+
	Still images	All subjects, including PE, Art and Music	6+
Chapter 6	The data projector		All ages
	PowerPoint		7+

1 Frameworks

This chapter contains the following activities

Many pupils find it hard to start writing. Many find it hard to continue. They are like gliders – often requiring a good deal of help to be launched – and, when airborne, still needing the thermals to keep them from descending. By providing support we can help them to fly. There are many terms for this: templates, writing frames, scaffolding, composition guides and so on.

While useful, such aids do have disadvantages, especially in printed form. They can act as a straitjacket and they can lead to formulaic writing. Presented in electronic form, they can be more easily adapted by or for individuals and allow pupils more choice and autonomy. Later in this book you will also find ideas to help get pupils launched

Activity 1: Narrative or autobiographical writing using starter texts

One of the simplest ways to get pupils writing is to provide them with a partially written text. This could be a starter paragraph:

> Fran looked at her brother. 'You did that on purpose,' she said. (etc)

One of the advantages of this kind of stimulus is that it doesn't 'begin at the beginning' but projects the writer straight into the story. Pupils often take too long to get to the point, believing that every story has to begin with a description of getting up and having breakfast.

However, it is more stimulating (because it is a challenge, a puzzle) to provide *two* paragraphs as a starting point, the task being to write the text which connects the two. This can be done on paper but a word processor has a number of advantages.

- the space between the paragraphs will expand to accept however much or little is written
- it will also accommodate narrative added before or after the paragraphs you have provided
- it will allow the writer to alter the text provided. Names of characters, or their gender can be changed, for example, as can settings, times and so on. This encourages a sense of ownership, autonomy and experiment.

In the following example, the names have already been made anonymous, in order to give the pupil more freedom.

> As soon as she could, _____ hurried along to the old house. What would she find when she got there? Would the door be locked? . . .
>
> . . . Suddenly, the sun broke into the darkness of the room. Its beams made the cobwebs look like little Christmas decorations. For a moment, the dust and dirt could be forgotten. There was _____. She was asleep.

Development and differentiation

Here are some variations on this approach.

- provide more demanding paragraphs
- provide three paragraphs
- set a particular genre as the style of the writing, e.g. horror, science fiction
- set a particular genre which is, on the surface, at odds with the nature of the paragraphs
- take paragraphs from stories which you intend to share with pupils later
- use paragraphs written by pupils themselves. This is a particularly good way to increase the self-esteem of pupils who do not see themselves as successful writers.

Activity 2: Writing to persuade or inform

This activity makes use of a traditional form of writing frame to guide pupils through a piece of persuasive or informative writing.

Example: Building up an argument

Using cars

> There are ….. adults in my family.
> We have ….. cars
> We use a car mainly to …
> Sometimes we could walk, for example, …
> We could also use a bus or a train to …
> If we did not have a car …
> I hope that when I grow up …

For those pupils without a car in the family

> There are ….. adults in my family.
> We do not have …
> We walk to …
> Sometimes we use a bus to …
> We go on a train when …
> If we did have a car …
> I hope that when I grow up …

It may be appropriate to complete some or all of the frame together before asking children to do their own, either individually, in pairs or small groups. It is useful to give *several alternatives* to demonstrate how different alternative versions can be – and to change some of the words presented by the frame to show that it should not be treated as carved in stone. The virtue of writing frames in electronic form is that they are malleable and pupils should be encouraged to alter them where they wish.

For example, one pupil might use the first frame to write this:

There are three adults in my family, my mum and dad and my gran. We have two cars. We use the car mainly to go to the shops and my dad uses the car to go to work because he works a long way away. Sometimes we could walk, for example, to school. We could also use a bus or a train but I prefer the car.

If we did not have a car I would be sad. I hope that when I grow up I will own a fast car which is red.

Another might adapt it thus:

There is one adult in my family and we have one car. My mum uses the car to take me to school and to get to work in Kingston. Sometimes we walk, for example, we go to the park and to my Auntie May's. We also use a bus or a train to visit my nana and gramps. I hope that when I grow up I will be able to afford a car and give my friends a lift.

If access to computers is severely limited, there is still value in completing the frame together (using a projector and/or interactive whiteboard) and then asking pupils do their own on paper.

Development and differentiation

You may wish to make two or more different versions for pupils of varying abilities. Ideally, the whole class will have looked at some simple examples of informative and persuasive writing. They will also have discussed some of the issues around car use, pollution and the environment.

As children's abilities increase, the persuasive element can be developed:

The curse of cars

In this country we use cars too much.

Cars are made from ...

Some bits of old cars are recycled but ...

Car engines use ...

The worst thing is exhaust fumes which ...

Exhaust fumes also ...

Some car journeys are essential, such as ...

On the other hand, ...

If we all used our cars a bit less, ...

We could do this by ...

Older pupils can cover similar ground but at a more sophisticated level, with only minimal support. Ask them to consider lighting, heating and entertainment; also conserving heat.

Saving energy

It is important that we all make an effort to cut down the energy we use because ...

There are many ways of doing this.

First, we could all ...

Secondly, ...

Also, ...

There are many other things we could do, including ...

Finally, ...

Within the same theme, similar outlines can be adapted for saving water and recycling rubbish.

Activity 3: Poetry patterns

While the forms and structures of poems may be obvious to us, they often have to be made explicit to pupils. Starting with the ridiculous, we may possibly move on to the sublime. Hence, this activity begins with the limerick and moves on to a simple four-line stanza form which is the basis of many traditional ballads and narrative poetry. The principle can be extended to deal with more complex poetic forms – or you can create new ones!

Example 1: Limerick lines

There was a young teacher at school
Whose class were delightful and …
They did all their …
Without shouting or …
And left her time to relax in the …

You may wish to present this as a word-processed document with rhymes from which they choose supplied beneath (or perhaps as a separate word list, see Hints and Tips, page 58.)
For lines 2 and 5: cool fool ghoul jewel mule pool rule tool wool yule
For lines 3 and 4: biting fighting lighting sighting writing

You may wish to provide the choice of words in this form:
For line 2: nice well-behaved canny cool wicked helpful clever dozy
For line 5: gym pub pool evening staff-room

To help organization, it may be preferable to place the words in a table. Again, see Hints and Tips (page 58) for more on this.

Development and differentiation

It might be a good idea to precede this activity with a look at existing limericks, which pupils can mark to show the rhyme scheme:

Once, on the River named _Esk_
Came a pupil on top of a _desk_
As he floated **ahead**
He smiled and he **said**
'It's unusual but quite pictur_esque_!'

As well as bold, underline or font size, they might like to use coloured text or the coloured highlighter. The latter is usually found near the font colour icon.
They can also clap out the rhythm and then mark the poem:

A <u>pig</u> with the <u>name</u> of Old <u>Sam</u>,
Said 'The <u>name</u> doesn't suit who I <u>am</u>.
I'd rather be <u>Bill</u>
Or Freddie or <u>Phil</u>,
But it's <u>better</u> than being called <u>Ham</u>.'

Don't be afraid to give them 'wrong' examples. They are an amusing way to talk about irregular forms:

Sean and his sister Siobhan
Did their best from the day they were born
They did what was needed
They writed and readed
But their spelling was always forlean!
      (or was it for phorlhan?)

Example 2: Simple as ABCB

This uses the rhyming pattern ABCB, one of the most common in narrative ballads and other poems. It also provides a template for the rhymes (ten down to none, as you will see) which helps by giving a clear aim. Because there is a lot of repetition, pupils could copy and paste to save writing out the repeated components:

Ten little schoolchildren
Standing in a line
One opened her mouth too far
And then there were nine

The instructions on Pupil Worksheet A (see page 60) may be useful. Alter them if it seems helpful.

Example 3: Finding and adapting patterns

Other poetry patterns can be adapted from poems and songs. This one is based on Roger McGough's poem, 'When to Cut your Fingernails':

Cut it on Monday
You'll hear scissors go snip

Cut it on Tuesday
You'll lose a hair grip

Cut it on Wednesday
It'll change into string

Cut it on Thursday
You won't feel a thing

(and so on)

These two are adapted from Kit Wright's 'The Magic Box':

My Special Bag

And what shall I put in my special bag?
The bag made of rags, the bag with a tag,
That says its name is Magi-Bag?

I shall put, from the land …
And a hundred …

I shall put, from the sea …
And a thousand …

I shall put, from the sky …
And a million …

That's what I'll put…. (optional repeat)

The Star of Gold

And what shall I put down in the hold?
The hold of my ship of oak planks old
That says its name is The Star of Gold?

I shall put, from the land …
And a hundred …

(and so on, as above)

Example 4: I am...

Finally, here is a classic method of creating imagery:

I am...

My hands are the end-twigs of the ash
They are knotted with veins

My hair is the coat of the grey wolf
It is rough from the sun and the rain

My eyes are the yellow lights of
They are …

My legs are …
They are …

My feet are …
They are …

My heart is …
It is …

Another approach might involve specifying a mood:

Sad I Ams

I am
the ring
from an empty soda can
the scrapings
from an unwashed porridge pan
the severed arm
of last year's Action Man

I am
the envelope
on which the gum is gone
the sticky tape
where you can't find the end
the gungy glue
that spoils instead of mends
the stamped addressed reply
that you forgot to send

I am
a garden
overgrown with weeds
a library book
that no one ever reads
a stray
which no one thinks to feed
the piece of good advice
which no one seems to need.

© Trevor Millum

Development and differentiation

All of these poetry patterns can form the basis of a satisfying collaborative writing session.

For example, read some lines from 'Sad I Ams'. Ask pupils to write some of their own. Give assistance where needed but, after five minutes, collect suggestions. If you have a projector, type and display the suggestions until you have ten or 12. In discussion you can then arrange them into another verse (or more, if you have the material) by selecting, moving and editing.

Some pupils will be happy to create their own poems in different moods ('Happy I Ams', 'Angry I Ams', etc.); others will prefer to work with the teacher or in small groups.

Activity 4: Using PowerPoint to present an argument

In many genres of writing, it is the underlying organization that presents most difficulties for pupils. Writing frames (as described previously, see page 3) can help to over come this. PowerPoint provides an alternative environment for organizing thought and, therefore, writing and speaking.

For any given topic, pupils can be provided with a number of slides on which the outline of the argument has already been entered. They might then be asked to add three or four bullet points to each one.

One of the advantages of this environment is that it encourages succinctness and order.

It should be noted that discursive and persuasive writing does not have to be based on adult preoccupations such as the environment, animal welfare or school democracy. Good practice in constructing logical texts can be gained in ways that are light-hearted and easier to grasp.

For example: the aim is to persuade your readers or listeners that Goldilocks should be punished severely.

Goldilocks: the case against

Goldilocks should be punished because...
- she caused damage
- she entered someone else's house
- she failed to say sorry
- she is selfish

She caused damage

She entered someone else's house

She failed to say sorry

She is selfish

Conclusion: a severe punishment is called for, because...

Image courtesy of Resource Education. Reproduced with permission.

Slide 1 states the case in summary. (Pupils may come up with other points, which can be inserted.) Slides 2–5 will take each of the main points and extend them. Slide 6 should restate the case and add a clinching argument!

The bullet points for each Slide 2–5 should offer supporting evidence and reasons why this behaviour is so bad. For example, Slide 3 might include:

* she entered the house like a thief
* discovering an intruder is very upsetting
* she helped herself to food and spoiled all the three dishes
* she lay on all the beds.

The bullet points should state the case clearly but without too much detail. When showing the slides, pupils can elaborate ('How would you feel if… ?').

Development and differentiation

A follow-up activity would involve a rebuttal. The argument might evolve as follows:

* she is only young
* the damage done is very small
* the house was open and inviting
* she has already been badly scared
* therefore, a suitable 'punishment' might be…

Further work could involve a discursive activity where pupils put the case for and against Goldilocks within the same presentation.

On the one hand, Goldilocks has…
On the other hand, the Three Bears should have…

Pupils may be able to suggest other cases for argument and debate, e.g. The Pied Piper of Hamlyn, the Little and Middle-sized Billy Goats Gruff, Beauty's father in *Beauty and the Beast*.

Finally

One area we have not touched upon in this chapter on Frameworks is mind-mapping. This is something often better drawn freehand on a flip-chart or marker board but it is worth considering software applications which can help pupils generate and organize ideas. There are a number of programs you can buy (type 'mind-mapping software' into a search engine) and some which are free and/or online. One that is free at the time of writing and which would be suitable for younger users (rather than business executives) is called Bubbl (without the 'e') and can be found at www.bubbl.us.

Whatever you choose, decide whether an ICT solution is appropriate and effective both in terms of time and cost – and that applies to all of the suggestions in this chapter and in the rest of this book!

2 Transformations

This chapter contains the following activities

Transformations involve making changes to existing texts. Through altering a piece of writing, pupils become engaged in thinking about language in a particularly focused way. It also enables them to work with language without spending time on writing which can often involve much more chore than creativity.

Activity 1: Sequencing

Most types of text have a logical sequence – it is part of the writing's coherence. Well constructed arguments, instructions, recounts and narratives all rely on a particular sequence either of sentences or paragraphs, or both. It is interesting to ask pupils to think of text types which do not display this characteristic, e.g. some poetry, some descriptions, a piece of advertising where the persuasive points are of equal weight, a shopping list.

Putting pieces of writing which have been desequenced back into their original order is therefore a very good way of learning about texts and how they are constructed. Doing this without ICT is awkward and frustrating, as many of us have learnt!

Ways of resequencing

There are several ways in which texts can be desequenced and resequenced:

- Word processors have various ways to cut and paste (tool bar icons, Edit menu items, keyboard shortcuts, drag and drop).
- Word has an especially neat shortcut. Select the sentence or line you want (experiment with triple clicking and clicking in the margin) and then use Shift, Alt and the up/down cursor keys. Magic!
- Some word processors (e.g. Textease) and publishing packages (e.g. Pagemaker) allow text to picked up and moved around the screen and placed wherever you wish.
- The software accompanying interactive whiteboards also allows you to move blocks of text around the screen.
- Words typed into an art package can be moved around like fridge magnets. Paint will allow you to do this, but be careful, it's easy to lose words or bits of them!

Example 1: Rhymes and jingles

Here is a simple poem to be resequenced. Pupils can be directed to look for clues in the rhyme pattern as well as the meaning of the piece. Model the process with pupils before asking them to sequence the same poem and then other, similar, poems. Let them build up confidence with, say, limericks before moving on to more demanding poetry.

The sky was dotted with stars
For he was only the farmer's boy
He lifted up the bars
She neither smiled nor thanked him
And she was the Jersey cow
They walked the lane together
Because she knew not how
They reached the gate together

(Anon)

Example 2: Narrative

Here is a desequenced paragraph from a story about a lad losing the football:

- Anyway, there was a hawthorn hedge and it would have hurt.
- But this time a woman answered the door straightaway.
- 'Hello?' she said. 'I don't want to buy anything.'
- I booted the ball and it shot into a garden three doors down.
- I hadn't met her before but there was something oddly familiar about her face.
- I went round the front, up the path and rang the bell.
- 'I'm not selling anything,' I replied. 'I just came to get our ball back.'
- It was the sort of bell you can't hear so you don't know if it works or not.
- 'Oh,' she said. 'Come in.'
- This time I didn't try getting over the back.

There are many linguistic features that help us to reconstruct the text: repetition from a previous sentence (e.g. 'It was the sort of bell…'), 'But' used as a connective, a pronoun referencing a character just introduced and so on. Overall, though, it is the feeling of 'rightness' (another way of saying 'coherence' perhaps) when the text is sequenced correctly which helps us.

It is the ability of ICT to allow us to try *different* sequences which makes this kind of activity effective and enjoyable. This is the original sequence. Bear in mind that slight variations in the sequence may still make sense and these can be good discussion points.

I booted the ball and it shot into a garden three doors down. This time I didn't try getting over the back. Anyway, there was a hawthorn hedge and it would have hurt.

I went round the front, up the path and rang the bell. It was the sort of bell you can't hear so you don't know if it works or not. But this time a woman answered the door straightaway. I hadn't met her before but there was something oddly familiar about her face.

'Hello?' she said. 'I don't want to buy anything.'

'I'm not selling anything,' I replied. 'I just came to get our ball back.'

'Oh,' she said. 'Come in.'

from *Gruesome Gran and the Broken Promise* by Trevor Millum.

Development and differentiation

Choose narrative texts for resequencing carefully and try them out yourself (or on a friend) before asking pupils to solve them. What seems terribly easy to begin with can be fiendishly difficult to the person coming to the text cold.

Rather than sentences, try sequencing a series of short paragraphs from a story. This will bring out different, though related, features of narrative texts.

Pupils can prepare texts for each other and they can be created from pupils' own writing too, as long as they exhibit enough features to make resequencing possible.

Example 3: Instructional writing

Instructions to make paper pop-ups

- Scoring makes for a much sharper and more accurate fold.
- Think before you glue.
- Score all the fold lines.
- Cut out the pop-up pieces.
- Sometimes flaps become inaccessible as the construction builds up.
- Having scored and cut out the pop-up piece, fold it along each crease and firmly run your finger nail along each fold.
- Measure and draw out the design.
- Then fold it back on itself and do the same thing again.

In instructional writing some stages must come before others. However, depending on the activity involved, there may be alternatives, so be aware of pupils who come up with a perfectly logical order which differs from the original.

Here is the above text in its original form:

1. Measure and draw out the design.
2. Score all the fold lines. Scoring makes for a much sharper and more accurate fold.
3. Cut out the pop-up pieces.
4. Having scored and cut out the pop-up piece, fold it along each crease and firmly run your finger nail along each fold. Then fold it back on itself and do the same thing again.
5. Think before you glue. Sometimes flaps become inaccessible as the construction builds up.

Development and differentiation

Useful texts of this type do not have to be complex. Even replacing an electric light bulb can be turned into a multi-stage operation.

- Switch on light to test.
- Remove old bulb.
- Locate new bulb.
- Dispose of old bulb safely.
- Switch off light.
- Insert new bulb.

There will be some alternatives – the old bulb could be disposed of before the new bulb is tested, for instance. Pupils will enjoy creating their own instruction lists and this is an ideal pair or small-group activity to develop thinking skills. It can be developed into a carousel activity as pupils move around from one computer to another to solve other groups' texts. A plenary session is then necessary in order to bring out the things that pupils found hard, to discuss ambiguities and review precision of expression. Don't forget to save any work created by pupils – it could be very useful next time.

Another area of interest might be the crucial work that verbs do in instructional writing. Do instructions always begin with verbs? Are they always imperatives?

Activity 2: Different audiences, different purposes

Reworking texts for different audiences or purposes is a time-consuming chore if traditional means are used. ICT enables pupils to focus on those parts of writing /rewriting/editing *that make a difference.*

Example 1: Yucky

Present a short text like the following and ask pupils to think about its possible purpose and audience.

> Slugs are loathsome creatures that lurk in damp unpleasant places, such as beneath stones or the under side of leaves. They eat all sorts of vegetable matter and are a menace in any well-kept garden. Slugs have a slime gland behind the mouth. This enables them to put down a yucky stream of slime over which to move. Disgusting!

Now ask them to edit the text so that it could be part of a factual description in a school library book called *Learning About Slugs and Snails*. When discussing the changes they have made, pay attention both to words that have been cut and words that have been replaced, e.g. 'unpleasant' can simply be removed but 'lurk' could be changed to make the description less negative.

Example 2: Yummy

Advertising text can be used in a similar way. How many purposes does this text have? Rework the following so that it describes only how to make the drink. How brief can the instructions be made?

Luxury hot chocolate drink

Indulge your love of chocolate with Cadbury's Velvet – the ultimate Hot Chocolate, made from flakes of Cadbury's milk chocolate. For a deliciously creamy drink add 6 heaped teaspoonsful (approx. 28g) of Cadbury's Velvet flakes to a large cup of hot milk. Stir the flakes until dissolved. Sprinkle a few more flakes on top of the drink before serving. For an even creamier drink, top your cup of Cadbury's Velvet with whipped cream and sprinkle more flakes.

Example 3: Cyclops

Is it possible to edit the following description so that the giant seems pleasant, or, at least, is presented neutrally?

The giant had a huge mouth containing some of the biggest, brownest, ugliest teeth in the world. They were like a wooden fence that had been battered by a storm, with bits missing and slanting at odd angles. They seemed to shake when the Cyclops roared. How well they worked, though! As the giant chewed, they crunched up whatever food it crammed in, smashing mutton bones to dust and crushing muscles and sinews like a massive mangle. Pieces of flesh and bone would fall from its rubbery lips onto the ground or cling to its cheeks and chin, stuck in the disgusting tangled beard like scraps of litter caught in ragged roadside trees.

Not easy, but possible with considerable alterations. You might begin like this:

The giant had a huge mouth containing some of the biggest teeth in the world. They were like a wooden fence with bits at interesting angles. How well they worked, though! As the giant chewed, they crunched up whatever food it put in very efficiently.

Perhaps it could be simplified for a younger audience and to be read aloud:

The giant had a huge mouth. In its mouth were some of the biggest, some of the brownest, some of the ugliest teeth in the world! Some were missing, some were slanting and some seemed to shake when the Cyclops roared. How well they worked, though! They crunched up the food it crammed in. They smashed mutton bones to dust. They mangled muscles. Crunch, crunch, crunch!

Activity 3: Just like fridge magnets

Example: 'Alphabet Soup' poem

a a a a a a a a an an ancient and and and and and and are ashore Atlantic baby beach belly black bluest box box box breakers broomstick Chinese colour corners cowboy dinosaurs dragon electric fashioned fifth fire first fish from from from from gold great Gujerati high rolling hinges horse I I ice in in in is its joints joke Lake Lucerne last leaping lid man my my night nostrils of of of of of of of of of on on on on on on on put rumbling sari season secrets shall sip smile snow spark spoken stars steel summer sun sun surf swish the the the the the the the the the then three toe tooth top touching uncle violet wash water white wild will wishes witch with with yellow

These are the words from a poem arranged in alphabetical order. (Instructions for how to do this will be found on the companion website.) Present this collection of words to pupils as a document file to use in their word processor. They can then use the words as if they were fridge magnets to create a piece of writing of their own. Drag and drop is the method most like using real fridge magnets and it is worth teaching pupils this skill if they are not familiar with it (see also Hints and Tips, page 58). Interesting images will be created, such as:

the wild violet dragon rolling on the white water
nostrils of fire and belly of silk
a cowboy baby from the great ancient surf

Pupils may well request additional words. You might turn them down unless there is a very good reason or relent if it is a preposition or relative pronoun. More interestingly, they will begin to ask if they can change words – for instance, to add an '-s' or an '-ed'. This attention to syntax should be encouraged! As this activity progresses, discussions about language arise naturally.

Development and differentiation

Any text can be used in this way. The nature of the original text will clearly affect the kind of writing which is possible. Experiment with different texts and with the kind of writing you ask pupils to produce. Does advertising text produce good material for poetry? Can persuasive or instructional texts ever really become anything else? Try it yourself and see! Here is the text from the packet containing powder for the luxury hot chocolate drink – this time with the maker's name omitted – shown on page 17.

approx. 28g 6 heaped a a a add an and before chocolate chocolate chocolate, chocolate cream creamier creamy cup cup deliciously directions dissolved drink drink drink drink even few flakes flakes flakes flakes flakes for for from hot hot hot indulge large love luxury made milk milk more more of of of of of of on serving. sprinkle sprinkle stir teaspoonsful the the the to top top ultimate until velvet velvet velvet whipped with with you're your

---

Activity 4: Plays and dialogue

Converting play script to prose dialogue (and vice versa) is a good way to focus on the conventions of each type of writing.

Example: Prose to play

The troll was woken up by the sound of hooves on his rickety-rackety bridge.

'Who's that trip-trapping across my bridge?' shouted the troll.

'It's only me,' said Little Billy Goat Gruff.

'Who's me?' said the troll.

'Little Billy Goat Gruff.'

'I like goat meat,' the troll cackled. 'I'm going to gobble you up for my tea!'

Little Billy Goat Gruff thought quickly.

'Don't do that,' he said. 'My brother will be along soon and he's much bigger.'

'Humm,' said the troll. 'How do I know you're telling the truth?'

'Look, here he comes now – over the top of the hill!'

'Go on then,' said the troll, licking its lips. 'I'll be ready for him!'

Little Billy Goat Gruff smiled and skipped over the bridge. 'Thanks, Mr Troll.'

Once the text is available as a document file, it can be transformed into play format quite easily without a lot of tedious copying. You might model the transformation so that it becomes:

The troll wakes up.

Troll: Who's that trip-trapping across my bridge?

Little BGG: It's only me.

Troll: Who's me?

Little BGG: Little Billy Goat Gruff.

Troll: I like goat meat. I'm going to gobble you up for my tea!

Little BGG: Don't do that. My brother will be along soon and he's much bigger.

It's up to you to decide how far to include stage directions such as '(shouting)' or '(angrily)'. Pupils can then carry out the changes themselves and complete the rest of the passage.

Development and differentiation

Carrying out the activity in reverse is more difficult. However, taken a step at a time it is something which many pupils can attempt.

Jack: (excited) Mum. You know those seeds.

Mum: I don't want to talk about them.

Jack: No, listen. You know I said they were magic...

Mum: (crossly) Magic! About as magic as my false teeth! And less use.

Jack: Have you wondered why it's so dark in here this morning?

Mum: It's cloudy.

Jack: It's not. The sun's shining.

Mum: (very irritated) What then?

Jack: Just come over to the window! Just come and look!

When modelling this transformation, manage the descriptions of speakers first, *then* put in the speech marks. Finally, add any other embellishments that pupils think will make the conversation sound better.

Activity 5: Making improvements

As writers we all know the importance of revisiting a piece of writing and making improvements to it. Very little of value is written without some reworking and often a final version is the result of considerable revision. This principle, though, is a hard one to embed in the practice of pupils. For one thing, it is quite a sophisticated aspect of writing and, for another, it's extremely tedious.

This latter disincentive, at least, can be overcome through ICT. A word-processed document can be revised without a complete rewrite. The text you are reading has been changed a great deal in the process of getting to a final manuscript. There have been deletions, substitutions and additions, paragraphs and sentences have been moved around, but the vast majority of the text did not have to be written out again.

Sharing the redrafting process

In order for pupils to get the idea of redrafting (or whatever you wish to call the process of improvement through making changes) it's useful to apply it to a short piece of writing, such as a poem or a short factual description. Once pupils have created a text in electronic form, perhaps using one of the suggestions in the previous section, share some examples with the class using a projector. Making sure to mention good points in the writing, discuss where improvements could be made, line order changed perhaps, or better vocabulary substituted. Model this a few times, involving pupils in the discussion. Then ask them to peer review each other's work and carry out some edits in a similar way.

> **Development and differentiation**
>
> Very valuable work on editing and improving can be done using a visualizer. Pupils do not have to have access to computers for this to be effective as they bring their writing on paper to the visualizer which then projects it onto the screen for the class to see. Using a highlighter pen or just an ordinary ball-point, teacher and pupils can pick out effective words and phrases, show suggested insertions, deletions and substitutions and use arrows to indicate where words or lines might be moved. One of the virtues of the visualizer, besides its simplicity, is the quality of immediacy: at any point, a piece of work (or anything else, for example, a poem from a book on the shelf, an article in a magazine) can be put under the lens and shown to everyone.

Finally

What all of these transforming activities have in common is a very precise focus on language. There may not be a great deal of writing to be done but there should be a lot of thinking, a lot of decision-making. And thinking about language is what we are trying to achieve in order to nurture good writers, readers, speakers and listeners.

3 Investigations and demonstrations

This chapter contains the following activities

ICT can be used to help pupils investigate language at word, sentence and text level – and a significant part of this involves the teacher using ICT to demonstrate language features. The projector (perhaps with interactive whiteboard) comes into its own again here. Changes that can be made to words, sentences and, indeed, whole texts that exemplify certain teaching points are hard to show using traditional means; even an OHP shows a static image.

The overlapping nature of our chapter titles is particularly obvious when we apply the technique of transforming a text into words in alphabetical order. The transformed text can then be used for a number of purposes, including an analysis of text types or genres or an investigation of word classes.

Activity 1: Investigating text types

Example: Matching text to type

Here are six texts in alphabetical order. Ask pupils to see if they can work out which is:

- part of a story
- a factual description
- an advertisement
- a council notice
- a book-cover blurb
- part of a menu

A

all and are are baked daily dough fresh freshest freshly hand-rolled highest in ingredients kitchens made on order our our pizzas premises prepared products quality the the to topped with with

B

a a all always among and and animals another are as be because become buildings catch chase clearly cracks damaged different eyes food for for from groups have have hunting in in large lifeline live making many mended move need of of one or own particular place plants prey remade see shapes silk silk spiders spiders spiders spiders spin the their their their their they they they they thread to to to to two use use very walls web webs webs when when

C

a a and and but crocodile designs granny happy has has has he him horribly is isn't Joe Joe look mean not of on only parents physically predatory repulsive rich she she suspects that the twelve-year-old uncaring unpleasant warden who

D

a all and and and are bechamel beef bolognese, cannelloni cannelloni cheese cheese creamy herbs in lasagne lasagne layered meat mushrooms, onions our parmesan pasta pastas rich salad sauce sauce sauce, served tomato topped vegetarian with with with

E

and and and and and apple as bark beneath cold collar concrete could could down dug earth face feet figgy first freshly from garden grass hands hear her her her her her her in into into jacket knobbly Laura lawn leaves of of of old on out own past pockets pulled reached second she she she she small smell smell soft squelch stepped steps the the the the the the the the the them then to touched tree turned up waited was went wind

F

about address advance and any arrangements as at at Bank collection collection day details director Environmental for have head Health help Holidays Housing I if in in in in indicated leaflet making may normal number of of or page phone please queries service Services shown shown smoothly tables thank the the the the the the the the these this this times to varied vary will work write you you your

This is an activity for which ICT is essential in preparation but which can be carried out on paper. Pupils should jot down their evidence for deciding on one type of text or another. At one extreme there are the ingredients from a menu; at the other might be the recognition that book-cover blurbs are often written in the present tense. All the pronouns in text E make it likely that it is a story and the superlatives in A point to promotional literature of some kind, and so on. These are only clues and we can never be sure; language is tricky and so are writers.

Instructions on using Word to prepare alphabetical texts are included on the website and on page 65 of this book.

Development and differentiation

Vary the difficulty of the text to suit ability levels. Pupils may like to collect their own short texts for reducing to alphabetical order. However, do not agree to type them all up yourself!

Present the words of a demanding text, perhaps a poem, in alphabetical form and allow pupils to create their own piece of writing from it. They will have opportunities to question unfamiliar words and to use them if they wish. In the next lesson, present the original text. It will have a ghostly familiarity and will, as a result of being previously experienced in a different form, be more intriguing and less daunting. For example, Blake's 'Tyger':

and and and anvil art aspire beat began brain bright bright burning burning burnt chain clasp could could dare dare dare dare deadly deeps did did distant down dread dread dread eye eye eyes fearful fearful feet fire fire forests forests frame frame furnace grasp hammer hand hand hand hand he he he heart heart heaven his immortal immortal in in in in its lamb made make night night of of of of on or or or see shoulder sieze sinews skies smile spear stars symmetry symmetry tears terrors the the the the the the the the the the the the thee their their thine threw thy thy thy thy thy to to twist tyger tyger tyger tyger was watered what what what what what what what what what what what what what what when when who wings with work

which you can present *without repeated words* if you prefer:

and anvil art aspire beat began brain bright burning burnt chain clasp could dare deadly deeps did distant down dread eye eyes fearful feet fire forests frame furnace grasp hammer hand he heart heaven his immortal in its lamb made make night of on or see shoulder sieze sinews skies smile spear stars symmetry tears terrors the thee their thine threw thy to twist tyger was watered what when who wings with work

(Note: Feel free to correct Blake's spelling of 'seize', though his version is the more logical, after all.)

Activity 2: Investigating word classes

You can use the same kinds of texts to look at word classes. Although this can be done on paper, it is a more stimulating activity on screen. Pupils can copy and paste (or drag and drop) words from the text into tables provided. This turns a rather tedious activity into one which most will enjoy. Trying to decide the class of a word out of context can be difficult, of course, and you may like to allow choices such as *adjective or noun* or *hard to decide* and allow words of three or fewer letters to be omitted.

again and and and around as as bare bark be cold could creature down earth feel feet from garden ground her her her hurried into it it jumper leaves Melanie moist more oak of of on out outline past pulled rotting rough she she she she she she shed shivered smelt soft squelch stairs stepped stretched tall the the the the the the the the the the thin tightly to touched toward tree turned under waiting was wild wooden would

This might also be done as a shared activity. Pupils might decide the following:

Adjective	Noun		Verb	Hard to decide	Don't fit (optional)
bare	bark	tree	could	rotting	again
cold	creature		hurried	squelch	around
moist	earth		pulled		down
more	feet		feel		from
rough	garden		shivered		past
shed	ground		smelt		tightly
soft	jumper		stepped		toward
tall	Melanie		stretched		under
thin	leaves		touched		
wild	oak		turned		
wooden	outline		waiting		
	stairs		would		

Development and differentiation

Give one half of the class the alphabetical text and the other half the original text and ask them to carry out the classification activity. You can then compare their results and look at those words that seem to depend on their function in the sentence to determine whether they are, for example, adjectives or nouns. One of the features of this text is the apparently small number of adjectives. 'Concrete' and 'apple' are not words we expect to be adjectives when seen in isolation, after all.

As Melanie stepped down from the wooden stairs on to the ground she could feel the soft earth squelch under her bare feet. It was cold and moist. She shivered as she stretched out and touched the rough bark of the tall oak tree. She hurried past it into the wild garden. She smelt the rotting leaves and turned toward the outline of the shed. Would the creature be waiting again? She pulled her thin jumper more tightly around her.

Tables like this can be used in any sorting activity, such as distinguishing common from proper nouns or present and past tenses.

Activity 3: Using codes to investigate words and contexts

Example: Code cracking

This is another activity that is simple to prepare using ICT and which can then be worked out using paper. Match the following encoded first words of nursery rhymes:

1. ◆◆Ж■&⋮●ℳ ◆◆Ж■&⋮●ℳ
2. ℳ◆○□◆⊠ ♫◆○□◆⊠
3. ℣ℳ□□℣Жℳ □□□℣Жℳ

    A. Humpty Dumpty   B. Georgie Porgie   C. Twinkle twinkle

To create a coded text:

1. Type (or copy and paste) the text and save it.
2. Do not use capital letters as they will be given a different code to lower case, making the job of the solver extra hard! (In most versions of Word, you can remove capitals by selecting all the text and pressing Shift and F3 which will cycle through capitals, lower case and 'sentence' cases.)
3. Leave an extra space or two between words – it helps pupils to see where the breaks between words occur.
4. Omit punctuation marks or they will be encoded too. It's better, if you need them, to add them in pen afterwards, before photocopying the completed worksheet.
5. Select all of the text (Ctrl A).
6. Change the font to a symbol font such as Webdings or Wingdings. Not all computers have the same ones but you are bound to have at least one suitable font.
7. *Make sure that words have not become split at the end of lines.*
8. Save your text using a *different* file name.
9. Get someone to try the puzzle just to ensure that it is possible to solve!

Development and differentiation

Depending on the text, you may wish to provide clues for pupils. For instance, you could give them all the vowels. Alternatively, discuss the passage together and ask questions like 'What is the most common letter in English?' Which one do you think it might be? When a certain number of symbols have been solved, let the pupils complete the rest of the passage.

Pupils may wish to create coded texts themselves. Make sure they have understood the instructions or the unlucky solvers may become unnecessarily frustrated.

There are a couple of coded texts for you to solve at the back of this book (see page 66). Tackling them will help you understand the processes children need to go through in order to reach a solution.

Activity 4: Peeking into texts

Example: The words that disappeared

This is another way of making work seem like play. Take a piece of writing which you wish pupils to examine closely. Type or paste it into a word processor and save it. Select all the text and change the colour of the font to white. Using a projector, show the invisible text. Double click anywhere in the text and a single word will be highlighted. Change the font colour to anything other than white and the word will be revealed, like this:

little

What kind of word might precede or follow this? Find out if you were right.

little spider

You can continue that investigation until a whole sentence has been revealed or dip in somewhere else altogether.

little spider   drainpipe.

(Once upon a time there was a little spider which lived in a dark old drainpipe.)

Development and differentiation

Show pupils how they can play this game with each other. How many words did they have to reveal before they recognized where the passage came from or the type of text it was? What gave them the clues? Were they misled at any point and, if so, why?

Activity 5: Sentence building

Example: Build it up, knock it down

Obviously, a word processor with a projector can be used to show sentence building. What is less often appreciated, is the power of 'unbuilding' using the Undo function.

For example, type a simple sentence: *The boy stroked the cat.*

Insert adjectives: *The lonely boy stroked the stray cat.*

Insert a phrase to describe the boy: *The lonely boy, dirty and dishevelled, stroked the stray cat.*

Insert a phrase or clause to explain time or place: *Having just rowed ashore, the lonely boy, dirty and dishevelled, stroked the stray cat.*

You can carry on like this (should you wish) until you have an outrageously unmanageable sentence, of course: *Having just rowed ashore, in a clinker-built boat of uncertain origin, the lonely boy, dirty and dishevelled (though not without a certain rakish charm), stroked – in an indolent way – the stray cat, which had been chasing (or rather, lying in wait for) mice all night.*

Pupils appreciate this kind of eccentricity once in a while.

However far you have taken your sentence, you can now return it to its original main clause by using Undo. If your word processor has a Redo function (as Word does) you may then *recreate* your sentence, expanding it bit by bit.

The dynamic quality of this kind of demonstration will appeal to pupils and will make clearer the way words build into phrases and clauses – and the way these then connect together to make complex sentences.

Development and differentiation

Ask pairs of pupils to create their own complex sentences, taking it in turns to add a word, phrase or clause. They can then present them and 'undo' them for others to see.

More able pupils can be given complex sentences to play with. Using a word processor, they can try to reduce them to the simplest main clause and then recreate them, either from memory or using Undo.

For example, they might gradually reduce the following sentence from this:

When she looked around her, she could see the eyes of the Wild Ones watching her and they were like the burning nuts of wood in the flames, gleaming with sparks.

to this:

she could see the eyes of the Wild Ones watching her and they were like the burning nuts of wood in the flames

and then to this:

she could see the eyes of the Wild Ones watching her

and finally to this:

she could see the eyes

before, of course, returning it to its full glory.

Activity 6: Moving and making

The word processor and projector can be used to demonstrate all sorts of other linguistic features, of course; for instance, making plurals, adding and changing prefixes and suffixes, altering tenses.

Example: A table of elements

Tables are a good way to organize such modelling. How many words can you make from these elements? You can drag (or cut and paste) the parts into the larger area to show the word and then use Undo to put them back again. Alternatively, you can then copy and paste to create new words and create a list of them in the cells underneath.

re	vent	ed
un	light	ment
pre	turn	en
de	speak	able
in	peat	s

If you're unsure how to create tables, see Hints and Tips (page 58).

Example: Spelling tricks

Certain spelling rules and conventions can be demonstrated in a visually arresting way using the sorts of programs listed in the sequencing activity in Chapter 2 (see page 14).

Using Word, you could show a series of possible letter combinations, asking pupils to identify the ones they think are correct. For example, type the following series of words, each time deleting the previous word (by highlighting it and pressing Delete or simply typing a new word while it is highlighted) before typing the next one:

lite   ligt   light   lihgt

Reveal the words one at a time by using Undo and/or Redo (the keyboard shortcut Ctrl + Z, Ctrl + Y is most efficient here) counting 1, 2, 3, 4. Pupils should jot down the number which represents the correct spelling. You could avoid any ambiguity by typing a number in front of each word:

1. lite   2. ligt   3. light   4. lihgt

To make this a more efficient activity, make the list ten or 12 words long. A variation would be to ask pupils to spot the wrong spellings. This is not appropriate for all children, of course. Those who have a very shaky grasp of spelling (for whatever reason) will simply find it confusing.

A PowerPoint version of this activity will be found on the accompanying website.

Activity 7: Investigating poetry features

As we know, the study of poetry can be reduced to a meaningless kind of simile spotting or alliteration alert. However, it can also be instructive, and fun, for pupils to see what they can discover in a poem (or, of course, any other piece of writing) as a part of understanding what makes different types of writing effective. Having listened to and/or read the poem opposite, pupils might work on it in pairs or small groups before sharing their findings as a whole class. Their investigation should inform and give depth to work in a further session where the poem as a whole, and others with similar themes, can be discussed.

The accompanying worksheet (Worksheet B on page 61) is one way of presenting this activity. It suggests that pupils decide on a favourite verse. The results can be tabulated on the board to see how far preferences are shared and the reasons pupils give for their choices. This can be a useful way into discussing the whole poem. Together with the worksheet, there is another example of a marked-up text, using 'Jabberwocky', which you may find useful to share with pupils.

'I saw the future far **away** –
Hearken friends to what I **say**!
I saw **grey night** and I saw **grey day**
In the future far **away**!

The Ballad of Unicorn Isle

Once upon a faraway time
Before the clocks had learned to chime
When every river spoke in rhyme
Once upon a time

Once within a distant land
Where mountains hadn't heard of man
Where dolphins played and bluebirds sang
Once within a land

Then and there in echoing light
Where gold was day and silver night
Lived unicorns of purest black and white
There in echoing light

One shining day in shimmering shade
The seer had come to speak they said
An ancient one with eyes of jade
One shimmering shining day

'I saw the future far away –
Hearken friends to what I say!
I saw grey night and I saw grey day
In the future far away!

I saw the pale two-legged beast
Rise up from west, rise up from east
And slay our kind for fun and feast
The pale two-legged beast.

It hunted down the unicorn
It cut off head, it cut off horn
Or stole our foals as they were born
And caged the noble unicorn.'

Once upon a desperate hour
In the shadow of the great moonflower
They made a pact to use their power
Upon a desperate hour

So faded they from human sight
Though wild geese see them from their flight
And children dream of them at night
Invisible to human sight

Once within a faraway land
Where unicorns first heard of man
Where hotels rise and tourists tan
Once within a land…

© Trevor Millum

Development and differentiation

This activity will work with texts of greater complexity (it has been used successfully with Keats' 'Eve of St Agnes', for example) or simplicity – try nursery rhymes or similar well-known songs and jingles.

As well as the verse from 'The Ballad of Unicorn Isle' a longer worked example will be found on the website. Bear in mind that this is just one person's response. Comparing different responses and perhaps combining them can make a fruitful plenary session.

Similar techniques can be used to annotate prose texts, whether fiction or non-ficiton. In fiction texts, pupils might also be looking for imagery, interesting (or difficult) words as well as phrases which build tension, add description to places or people and so on. In non-fiction texts, pupils could pick out the most important facts in one way, subsidiary ones in another, together with a third option marking language which is not fact, but opinion. For example, using the description of slugs on page 17, where bold = negative opinions, underline = basic facts and italics = subsidiary information.

<u>Slugs</u> are **loathsome** creatures that <u>**lurk** in damp</u> **unpleasant** <u>places</u>, *such as beneath stones or the under side of leaves*. <u>They eat all sorts of vegetable matter</u> and are a **menace** in any well-kept garden. <u>Slugs have a slime gland behind the mouth</u>. <u>This enables them to put down a</u> **yucky** <u>stream of slime over which to move</u>. **Disgusting**!

Finally

Once again, you will notice that the emphasis has been upon examining words closely, often in a context which makes the study of language a pleasure rather than a chore. A hidden or invisible message is always more interesting than a visible, obvious one, a dynamic activity more engaging than a static one. ICT is very good at helping us to provide these and to tailor them to our particular needs.

4 Communication

This chapter contains the following activities

ICT is renowned for its powers of communication. For the teacher of English, however, it is usually more important to have something to communicate than to worry about the means of communication. Nevertheless, different forms of communication require different skills and impose different conventions on what is said or written.

Communication using ICT can function in one or all of three ways:
- publishing
- researching /receiving
- peer-to-peer

or, more briefly: up, down and sideways. In internet terminology, this might be described as uploading, downloading and exchanging.

Activity 1: Publishing

Publishing pupils' work on paper is expensive and takes a lot of time to prepare. Publishing electronically is cheap and, once you have a system or template established, much less time-consuming.

The most obvious place to publish children's work is on the school website. Any school that is proud of its pupils' writing should automatically have an area in which to display it. Some schools do this by year group or by class names.

There are professional websites which publish children's writing but they vary in quality and there you have little or no control over how they are displayed or for how long. However, it is worth checking if your local authority or your regional 'grid for learning' offers this opportunity. If not, you might ask, why not?

While your pupils' writing will not (in spite of the hype) reach a world-wide audience, it can reach a substantial and important audience comprising parents and other relatives, governors, local people and other schools.

Example: The review file

The simplest ideas often work best. Divide the class into small groups and ask each group to select a book, a film and a TV programme that they like. Tell them that they have between 60 and 80 words to:

1. describe the book, film or programme
2. give their opinion on it
3. give the reasons for their opinion.

If opinions differ they must say something like: 'Some of us thought that… Others felt…'

After a maximum of ten minutes' discussion, they should type up their reviews, doing word counts from time to time. For example:

Film: *Harry Potter and the Chamber of Secrets*. This is the second Potter film and tells how Harry and his friends discover the hidden chamber. The baddies are the same as in the first film with some new monsters like giant spiders and the huge serpent. We thought it was exciting and interesting. There are some good special effects and the story keeps you wondering what will happen next. (69 words)

It doesn't matter if the same item gets reviewed by more than one group. The comparisons can be revealing. Sometimes they can be combined – a useful exercise in itself.

Save each review as a separate file in a folder labelled 'Website Reviews'. When you come to upload them (or pass them to the ICT Co-ordinator to do so) they need to be easily identifiable. Several files named 'Harry Potter and the Chamber of Secrets' are not as easily managed as 'Harry1', 'Harry2' and so on.

Development and differentiation

Some groups may need a writing template to help them (see Chapter 1) and some may not complete all three reviews. Pupils may wish to write other reviews in their own time in the weeks that follow. The pages thus created will form a useful resource for other classes and, indeed, other schools.

Remember

Points to bear in mind when putting pupils' work on the web:

- Your own school website is the most suitable place. If you use professional sites, be prepared to wait for work to be accepted.
- Work should be changed often and then archived.
- The writing you publish should be varied, not just poems and stories. Reports on school activities are interesting and useful.
- Writing should be fairly short but variety of length is good.
- Try to keep a reasonable age and gender balance.
- Pictures (simple, not memory hungry) always help to lighten a page.
- Spelling and other mistakes do not help your school's image so proofreading is even more important than usual!
- People only know your pupils' work is there if you tell them so traditional means of promotion are still important: a note in the letters home, posters in Reception or a mention in the local paper will all help.
- Writing for publication is a great motivation, so don't let the pupils down. Be realistic about what can be achieved.
- Web publishing can be an ongoing activity or a one-off special.
- Take account of the school's e-safety guidelines.

Activity 2: Researching

Teachers will be familiar with the pros and cons of using the internet. Apart from concerns about children accessing unsuitable content, the time spent trying to find what you want in a form which is useful can be counter-productive. There is also the danger of the Thoughtless Topic Syndrome whereby pupils download words and pictures and paste them into their work without understanding (or sometimes even reading) the material they have gathered, much as they did in the past when copying material from encyclopedias and other reference books.

Time is often better spent searching within a known site such as the BBC or KidZone where you know the content will be relevant and at an appropriate level. However, it is essential that pupils know how to sift material and select intelligently. In this activity they are not so much looking for specific information as making judgements about the *quality* of the sites visited.

Example: Rating websites

Pupils are asked the question:

Imagine you are writing a speech to persuade people to conserve/use less energy. How would you rate the following sites?

www.est.org.uk/home (tip: click on 'green communities')

www.alliantenergykids.com

http://www.etsu.co.uk/ (click on side bar 'renewable energy for kids')

www.epa.gov/recyclecity/

www.eco-schools.org.uk

Provide pupils with a checklist or table along the lines of the one below – but encourage them to add their own comments, like 'The first page was good but the rest was hard to understand'.

Website:

	Very	Quite	OK	Not very	Not at all
How easy is it to understand?					
How useful for your purpose?					
How reliable do you think it is?					
How easy is it to find what you need?					
Other comments					

Remember that websites can change and that the URLs (their unique addresses) can alter. Check any websites before use, especially those recommended in printed texts like this one. You will almost certainly find other useful ones to include in your list. This response form is included at the back of the book (see page 67) and may be photocopied.

Development and differentiation

Information gleaned from this task could indeed provide the material for writing the speech as a persuasive text or a balanced report on energy conservation by ordinary people (i.e. individual home/garden/travel use).

You may wish to download and print out certain web pages to use as examples. Pupils can be encouraged to annotate them with questions and comments. Enlarge one on the photocopier so that you can give examples of the sorts of things worth pointing out.

Activity 3: Exchanging

In the last few years Web 2.0 applications such as YouTube, Facebook and Twitter have opened up huge possibilities for people to exchange information rather than simply to receive it. These social networking sites are often blocked by educational institutions but there are other internet-based ways of peer-to-peer communication which can be used very effectively in schools. Sites such as Wikispaces offer the facility to share ideas and to have discussions that open up interesting possibilities, especially for those who do not always take part in class discussion. In addition, the school VLE (or 'learning platform') should provide an effective and safe environment for exchange. The example that follows could be adapted to suit that environment.

Email is another underused aspect of ICT in the classroom and yet it opens up opportunities for writing for different audiences that are hard to achieve by other means.

Example: e-stories

This activity depends upon finding a partner with whom to communicate. It could be another class in your school or in another school. A school in another country would be interesting. Another possibility is an adult such as a governor, a parent or a writer.

Once a partner has been established, you can start to write a story together. Sequels make a good starting point. I have been involved with pupils writing sequels to *Carrie's War* (this time set in Scotland) and *Mrs Frisby and the Rats of NIMH* (describing the Frisby family's expedition to the rats' new home).

One class writes the first few paragraphs and then emails them to the other class. They have to continue the story and then send it back. The story-writing continues in relay until you agree that it's time to bring it to a conclusion.

The activity requires shared writing, which is not always easy to manage. However, the motivation involved in this kind of project usually ensures a high degree of co-operation. One of the best methods seems to be:

1. Discuss the characters
2. Discuss the general direction the next part of the story is going to take
3. Brainstorm words and phrases that might come in useful
4. Using a projector, teacher acts as scribe while pupils suggest what to write
5. The passage is edited and improved and then saved
6. With a final check, it is attached to an email and despatched
7. Wait expectantly…

When the next episode arrives, it can be displayed in the same way or printed out and duplicated as it is sometimes useful for pupils to have their own copy to refer to. 'The story so far…' always needs to be read carefully so that the next episode will have no errors in continuity or characterization.

This kind of activity has a number of virtues:

- it is very low cost and very low tech!
- it achieves a high level of motivation
- it gives pupils a reason to read and reread a text carefully
- it provides a different (and real) audience and purpose.

It also enables you to model writing as an organic process, i.e. where creating and editing, correcting and improving can occur as the writing proceeds, rather than as separate activities.

Development and differentiation

The shared writing can be carried out in a number of ways. Groups of pupils can write the next episode and the pieces can then be compared, the best bits from each being used. This is time-consuming but worth doing once, especially if each group's work is saved on disk or on the network. Showing how parts of different texts can be combined is a very useful skill to demonstrate – and one in which pupils will be only too happy to participate.

If you have agreed a structure for the episode – e.g. description of Jamie's house; his conversation with his aunt; walking to the station and missing the train; dialogue with the railway staff; deciding what to do next – then it is possible for each group to write one of the sections, which you can then easily combine. This works well if you only have access to one computer, as it does not have to be done simultaneously.

Finally

We all know that learning takes place when pupils are engaged in doing rather than in watching or listening. The more they are active participants in the communication processes, the more they will learn. Their involvement in publishing and in peer-to-peer exchanges will be self-evident but helping them become proactive and critical users of the internet is equally important.

Pictures and sound

This chapter contains the following activities

The opportunities to use pictures as well as words have multiplied over the last few years. In addition, the *ease* with which images, still and moving, can be created, manipulated and integrated into literacy work has increased even more dramatically. Simplicity and ease are crucial, given the pressures on time and on access to equipment: it is essential that hardware and software are straightforward to use.

While pictures are not obviously the province of teachers of literacy, the teacher concerned is also likely to be the teacher of everything else, including art and ICT. What, then, can images contribute to the teaching of literacy?

Activity 1: Film

Children of all ages can make films. However, there is more to making a film than pressing the record button – and this is where literacy comes in.

Example: Film your topic!

Researching and planning

Whatever the class topic happens to be, pupils can be asked to research different aspects of it. Break the topic down into smaller chunks so that each group of four or five has a manageable task. For example, if the topic was volcanoes, some separate aspects might be: famous volcanoes, what causes volcanoes, the most recent eruptions, Pompeii, extinct volcanoes and so on. Here they will need guidance as in any piece of research (see Activity 2 in Chapter 4, page 40).

Explain that if they wish to produce a good piece of film, pupils will need to come up with some basic facts and then decide how to present them. Different means of presentation might be re-enactment, interview, reporter 'on the spot' or straight to camera. Once they have some information and have decided their approach, the best way to organize their material is through creating a storyboard.

Storyboards

An A3 sheet divided into eight or 12 rectangles can be drawn by pupils or photocopied. Pupils draw simple outlines of what should be shown in each section or cut and paste real pictures. They then add a brief description together with the *words that are to be spoken*. Getting this part of the activity right is the key to the success of the whole project and is worth taking time over. It is probably worth having a trial run as a whole class, using the interactive whiteboard to demonstrate how to create an effective storyboard.

Once the storyboards are complete, pupils can use them to create their scripts. When they start filming, the storyboard together with a copy of the script will guide the 'director'. Those who are acting/presenting need to learn their lines. However, unlike a play, a film can be created in separate pieces and can be re-recorded. As a result, those with a poor memory or who lack confidence can speak their lines a small part at a time.

Filming

Allocate the following responsibilities: director, camera operator, actors. It may be that you wish to retain the role of director, at least to begin with.

Any camera with video facilities can be used, although obviously you will get a higher quality end-product with a more expensive camera. While a good-looking film is important (it shows pupils and all future audiences that the work is valued), it is not the most important issue. After all, a great poem can be produced on a cheap typewriter.

At this stage of production, speaking and listening become paramount. Pupils need to try out their work, then rehearse their lines more formally and finally speak them clearly and with appropriate tone and emphasis while the camera is rolling. Again, a trial run with volunteers will throw up examples of good and bad practice: speaking too quietly, too fast, in an unsuitable tone and so on. Almost all pupils will respond to coaching and exhortation and be pleased with themselves when you can compliment them: 'That's it! Wasn't that a whole lot better? Excellent…' rather than accepting a sub-standard performance.

As teacher, you will want to direct and film the trial run. You will be able to remind them to look at the camera (if it is a 'straight to camera' piece) and not to swing their arms or move about. It's important that performers stand or sit in the same place and do not wander about. It means you can later edit their performances without their heads or bodies jumping from one place to another!

When pupils start to handle the cameras themselves, they will forget some of the guidelines you have established but the resultant films will provide a good reminder.

Editing

The editing stage is the most demanding and it is important to become familiar with the software you are going to use beforehand. Most programs involve importing your film clips from the camera, selecting the ones you want to use and then dragging them onto some form of timeline or storyboard. The amount of editing which can be done varies but all programs will allow you to crop film clips to remove unwanted parts. As with a word processor, you can cut, copy, paste, copy and delete. However, unlike a word processor, you cannot add new material without getting the camera out again! Always take more film than you think you will need. And always save your work as you go along.

Once you have a 'rough cut' of your film, you can improve it by adding or altering the transitions between clips, adding a music track, captions, title and credits. If there's anything pupils love, it's credits – so don't overlook them. As with PowerPoint, pupils also like to play with special effects such as the way text appears on screen or disappears from it. Leave time for this.

Viewing

Finally, you have the showing of the film or films, firstly to the makers and afterwards, one hopes, to a wider audience. In reality, this is not the final stage because you should really hold a debriefing. But that should be deferred to another day. For the moment, enjoy the show.

The literacy component

It will be clear from the outline description of the film-making that it has involved a lot of literacy activities: both purposeful reading and writing (in the research and scripting/storyboarding stage) and speaking and listening (not just in the rehearsal and performance, but in all of the task-based talk which contributes to the project). The next time you do it, it will be even better!

Development and differentiation

Many of the opportunities for differentiation here will centre on the amount of responsibility given to pupils. Some will need close guidance, perhaps working though a series of numbered instructions; others will be self-directed. Do not underestimate the abilities of those who do not normally shine in literacy work. Film-making can often enthuse and motivate them.

A natural development of this work is to create resources which will be used by other classes, now and in the future. The resources might be stored on the school's learning platform for use by teachers or on the school website, freely available to the public. If the purpose of a film is to teach something (rather than just to entertain) pupils will learn to approach the task in a different manner.

Activity 2: Animation

As with filming, animation can be used to support any kind of work. It's popular with children and is a powerful medium. It is also very time-consuming.

Example: A twist in the traditional

Some very good work can been done re-telling traditional stories, often with a slight twist to them. Much of the preparation will be similar to the process described in the previous activity, without the need for research. The story will have to be broken down into short scenes and a list of backgrounds, props and characters made. You may decide to make your own characters or use existing ones (e.g. Lego, Playmobil, etc.) depending on time available. Backdrops can be painted or collaged, giving a real purpose to some large-scale artwork.

There are a number of software packages suitable for younger children. They will all depend on taking many shots and making small changes in the position of characters and any other moving items. You will soon understand why 'stop frame' animation is very time-consuming – but fascinating. The more pictures you take, the smoother your film will look.

The software will combine your pictures into an animated film which you can, as with simple filming, edit as described above. With most films, speech is part of the filming. With animation, it is added afterwards. This offers a very focused opportunity (and necessity) for clear speaking. Your audio track can be edited alongside the animation so that they synchronize. If pupils learn to do this themselves they will acquire all sorts of skills along the way, including making subtle changes to the story to fit what appears on screen!

Once again, you will want to add titles, credits and, possibly, captions within the film. In some cases, a music track may be appropriate; just ensure that it is not overpowering.

Development and differentiation

It is, of course, possible to mix animation with film. A film to explain a scientific process, for example, might include a piece straight to camera followed by a short animation to illustrate the point.

Try to develop pupils' abilities to remember their lines and to improve their delivery. Seeing themselves on screen is an effective way to demonstrate both shortcomings and good technique. Your class could get together to produce a short humorous film which demonstrates all the things which can go wrong, including mumbling, looking off camera and fidgeting.

Activity 3: Still images

Powerful as moving images are, the still image can also be a very effective – and quicker, cheaper – alternative. Still images taken with inexpensive digital cameras can be transferred to the computer quickly and adapted to many teaching and learning situations. For example:

* Artwork made by pupils can be integrated into their written work.
* Any kind of learning activity with a visual component (e.g. a science lesson) can be photographed and the images used as part of a display or in pupils' reports.
* Pupils can take pictures of each other depicting different moods and feelings.

Example: All about me

A class of six–seven-year-old children are divided into groups and each group given a digital camera. They have to take photos of each other and each pupil has to tell the group four facts about him or herself. These can be as varied as favourite colours, where they live, what hobbies they have or whether they have brothers and sisters. The cameras are then collected and the images loaded onto a computer.

A simple program such as PhotoStory can be used to display the pictures as a slide show. Then you need to add the soundtrack! Divide the groups into pairs and get pupils to practise interviewing each other. This is where they will tell each other some of the facts they've already discussed. Record each pair and attach the facts about each pupil to their picture. You can adjust the amount of time the picture is displayed so that it coincides with the time taken by their recorded speech.

Some pupils will need a number of 'takes' before they say their words distinctly; reassure them that this is all right and that hesitations and gaps can be edited out later. The result is a collage of everyone which will amuse and entertain both your class and many others. In the process, children will have learnt to select information, to talk with their peers and to speak clearly.

Development and differentiation

The software used to display the images and sound will usually offer the opportunity to add captions and titles. The use of captions requires pupils to become adept in summary and precision: very useful literacy skills. You can capitalize upon this without necessarily taking the time to create your own photographs. Within a given topic, pupils can research and download images, import them into the software and add their own captions to explain their relevance to the topic. Sound does not always have to be added; omitting it can make pupils focus more on the words which will appear on screen; it also does away with the need for complete quiet!

Finally

In general, pupils are very enthusiastic about using both still and moving images. As a result, their expectations can sometimes outstrip their abilities or the time and equipment available. Help them to learn the virtue of achievable goals! Further, never lose sight of your own literacy goals: there will be no shortage of opportunities to develop not just speaking and listening, but also reading and writing, to say nothing of team-working, problem-solving – and patience.

6　Presentations

This chapter contains the following activities

We have seen, in the previous chapter, how the presentation of images can contribute powerfully to literacy teaching and learning. We all know that ICT provides us with powerful presentational tools. Indeed, one might be forgiven for thinking that this was ICT's main function. Many teachers' experiences have been restricted to death by bullet points in PowerPoint or the use of word processors or desktop publishing (DTP) packages to make work *look* good.

There is a place for looking good. Pupils appreciate having their work displayed professionally without the demotivating effect of poor handwriting. Having the goal of producing, say, a page for a class magazine or display can focus minds and improve the quality of proofreading. Teachers, also, like being able to produce good, clear worksheets; there is now no excuse for poor quality resources.

However, we all know the danger of valuing presentation over content. A word-processed essay is not a better essay – it is just easier to read. Hence, there is little educational value in typing out an already hand-written piece of writing. (Pupils will often undertake this very happily as it involves no thought on their part but *seems* to be achieving something of great value!)

PowerPoint can, of course, be used for its primary function. It can help pupils to organize their thoughts when preparing a talk, for example. The 'slide sorter' view which shows all the slides on screen at the same time is a good way to review ideas and structure. The slides can be moved about just like words in a word processor, so adjusting the structure is easy, as is adding new points or removing/editing existing ones. (See Activity 4 in Chapter 1, page 10.)

That having been said, there are other ways of using presentational tools which offer interesting opportunities for learning.

Activity 1: The data projector

With or without an interactive whiteboard, the data projector (also known as an LCD projector or video projector) offers enormous scope for teaching and learning in English. Many examples have already been given throughout this book.

As with the internet, so with presentational devices: they can be used in at least two ways: pupils can use them as well as teachers and this use by their peers will often have more impact on fellow learners.

The projector can be a very powerful tool in conjunction with your word processor. Some specific examples were given in Chapter 3. In particular you might like to think about the further possibilities offered by:

- revealing hidden (white on white) text (Activity 4)
- undo and redo (Activity 5)
- marking texts with the highlighter (Activity 7).

Another simple feature in Word which is useful in this context is the ability to enlarge a word or a phrase quickly and dynamically.

Should you be working on a text where you wish to draw attention to a particular word, select the word and then hold down Ctrl and Shift. While they are held down, press the greater than key (>). The word will enlarge before your (and their) eyes. Ctrl + Shift + < will reduce it again. Ask pupils to come to the computer to demonstrate any language features in this way and you will have plenty of volunteers.

Finally, don't forget the many ways in which sequencing can be used to focus minds on different aspects of a text and the keyboard shortcut for moving sections of text (see Chapter 2, Activity 1 on page 14).

Activity 2: PowerPoint

PowerPoint has been so (over)used to make training presentations that its more creative possibilities are often overlooked. Here are a few suggestions which you may find helpful in literacy teaching and learning.

Example 1: Spelling patterns

Use the Custom Animation feature of PowerPoint to make the letters of, say, 'ight' words, appear one at a time ('flash once, slow'), together with a suitably arresting (or irritating) sound effect.

Another example would be to display nouns ending in 'y' with plurals, using the 'crawl from left' animation option.

Example 2: Sorting

Pupils can use PowerPoint in its 'create' or 'edit' mode (rather than as a presentation) to move words and phrases around the screen. This is an ideal way to sort into categories, e.g. comparatives and superlatives, active and passive. Once they have done this, they can learn to create their own sorting activities for others:

> Arrange these words to make a sentence:
>
> Hills   of   popular   Cotswold
>
> tourist   the   most
>   the
> destinations   are   one

To move a word, click on it to bring up the surrounding text box. Click the mouse pointer onto the frame of the box and a four-way arrow will appear. The box can then be dragged around the screen and repositioned in the usual drag-and-drop manner. See Hints and Tips (page 58) for further advice.

Development and differentiation

Less able pupils may find that reconstructing a sentence like the one shown above is too difficult. They may still benefit, however, from recreating the sentence: just leave the target sentence showing at the top and ask them to make a copy of it. More able pupils can be challenged by two sentences jumbled on the slide. More than two becomes awkward and crowded but experiment – and, even better, let them experiment.

Example 3: Poetry interpretations

PowerPoint has many ways of displaying and introducing words. These features can be used to present and interpret existing poems in interesting ways and to display pupils' own writing.

In the example above, a pupil who has written a very short description and does not even recognize it as a finished piece of work can begin to appreciate how even a few words can be very effective. Pupils can also discuss whether the 'poem' would be better arranged in a different way:

The hawk circled
Like a carousel
In the sky

or perhaps:

The hawk circled
In the sky
Like a carousel

You can also discuss presentational devices: which font is the most suitable? How should the words be arranged on the slide? How should they move onto the screen: circling, crawling from left or right, silently appearing? PowerPoint offers so many alternatives! And should there be any accompanying sound effects? Would it be enhanced with an illustration – or would that be a distraction?

Ask pupils to look through their previous writing to see if they can find an example of fewer than, say, 16 words which could be displayed in a similar way. A collection of such short pieces would make a powerful presentation or foyer display.

Example 4: Flying texts

Display a short text so that the words appear and then disappear. You will notice that punctuation marks seem to gain unusual prominence through being momentarily isolated. Words which we normally pass over without noticing are given a more equal weight. These and other factors affect the way we 'see' the text. What words do we recall? What deductions can we make about the text type? What predictions? How far can we, as a class, recreate the text?

> ### Development and differentiation
>
> As is usually the case, pupils learn more if they are actively engaged. With this in mind, it is worth spending time getting them to create some of the presentations described in this chapter. Pupils who create their own teaching presentation to try and get across a spelling difficulty, for example, are more likely to remember the information than those who merely view it. Similarly, pupils can be asked to create slide shows, or the equivalent, which present poems (or verses of poems) in appropriate ways. In this situation, discussion afterwards should focus on how suitable and thoughtful the presentation was. The aim should be to develop from merely illustrating a text with obvious images to creating mood or even subverting the text. If this last suggestion seems too demanding, just think about illustrating the verse about 'quinqueremes from Nineveh' in John Masefield's 'Cargoes' with a picture of galley slaves pulling at their oars...

Finally

One of the great values of presentation is the esteem which it can bestow on pupils, the value which it can give to their work. Praising a child's work is good; issuing a grade can be useful, but showing an audience something a pupil (or group of pupils) has created demonstrates positive feelings in a way that is powerful and real.

Conclusion – why it's worth it

You have probably not read this book from cover to cover. More than likely you have dipped in and made use of ideas where they have fitted your most immediate needs. However, I would advise you to have a look through chapters you may have skipped and to think about what it is that makes ICT so useful (as well as sometimes infuriating) in the teaching and learning of literacy.

One of the key things must be flexibility or malleability. Whichever term you use, the underlying principle is that you can easily change things – and keep your previous effort too if you wish. ICT offers the opportunity to try things out, to experiment and to get things wrong. These opportunities to use trial and error (or iterative learning) are particularly valuable because they are so rare in other modes of teaching and learning.

ICT also offers great possibilities for sharing, whether it's teacher with class, class with other classes/schools, pupils with each other or teachers with each other. Make use of this collaborative aspect and you and your pupils will all benefit.

What you will also have noticed is that ICT encourages a very precise focus on language. In activities involving transformation, investigation or organization, there may not be a great deal of writing taking place, but there will be a lot of thinking, a lot of decision-making and often a good deal of discussion. Writing for its own sake does not serve an educational purpose – often the opposite!

Further, we all know that learning takes place when pupils are engaged in doing rather than passively watching or listening. Doing for themselves – making their own sequencing activity, their own table of word classes, their own little animation is a key ingredient in learning. We all know that we learn and remember when we are actively engaged in doing something – and doing something we enjoy.

Finally, though, never lose sight of your literacy goals – and if quiet reading, drama, pencil and paper or anything else will do the job better, use it!

Hints and tips

These apply specifically to Word but you are likely to find similar functions in other word processors.

Multiple windows

It is possible to have more than one text window available on screen at the same time. This is useful if you want to display a word list or glossary or even to compare different texts alongside each other. Click on the middle of the three icons at the top right of your text window to allow multiple windows. The icon will look slightly different according to your operating system and the screen resolution.

You can then resize them to suit the work being done. For example, a word list may require a long thin window. Pupils can then cut and paste or drag and drop words from the word list into their own writing.

Tables

In all versions of Word, there is an facility to insert a table into your document. You may have a Table menu visible or you might need to use the Insert menu, depending on the version of Word. Once you get to the option to Insert Table you can determine the number of rows and columns you require. The table can be edited if you decide you need a different layout later. To make columns wider or narrower, click on any of the uprights and drag it to the left or right. Each cell will enlarge itself to accept whatever amount of text you wish to insert. The tab key can be used to move you from one cell to the next. There are many more things which can be done with tables, of course, but this is a start.

Drag and drop

This is the most effective way of moving small amounts of text around (or pictures and other items in applications such as PowerPoint). If your pupils have not mastered it, it is worth teaching them.

Select the text to be moved. (A single word can be selected with a double click, a paragraph with three clicks, a line by clicking in the margin.) Point the mouse into the highlighted area and the caret will turn into a pointer again. Press the left mouse button and keep it pressed down. Move the mouse until the tip of the arrow points to where you wish to deposit the text. (A faint upright line will show the position.) Release the mouse button.

You might like to use these instructions in a sequencing exercise, but do check them out first!

Make bigger

Don't forget the little technique mentioned in Chapter 6, Activity 1 (see page 52) whereby you can make words bigger (and smaller) instantly by using Control, Shift and the greater than/ lesser than keys. Select the word or words first, hold down Ctrl + Shift and then hit < or >. You can keep your finger on these latter keys and watch the word(s) grow or shrink before your eyes.

Move up, move down

Remember also, the way you can swiftly move lines or paragraphs swiftly through a text. Position your cursor anywhere in the paragraph and then hold down Shift and Alt. Use the Up/Down cursor keys (sometimes called the arrow keys) to move your selection. If you wish to move a single line, make sure you have separated it from the surrounding paragraph by pressing Enter before and/or after it.

PowerPoint words

If you're wondering about entering lots of words in different places on the screen as suggested in Chapter 6, try this method. Insert a text box and type all the words you will want. Then, word by word, or phrase by phrase, select and drag text out of the text box somewhere else on the slide. Each will form its own little text box.

Pupil worksheet A

Writing your own 'Ten Little...' poem

1. Open your word processor
2. Start a new document
3. Type the following:

    Ten little schoolchildren
    Standing in a line
    One opened her mouth too far
    And then there were nine

4. Save the document
5. Copy these four lines and paste them underneath, leaving a gap of one line.
    To copy: select the four lines
              click on the Copy icon
              click to put the cursor where you want it
              click on the Paste icon

    It should now look like this:

        Ten little schoolchildren
        Standing in a line
        One opened her mouth too far
        And then there were nine

        Ten little schoolchildren
        Standing in a line
        One opened her mouth too far
        And then there were nine

6. Now change some of this verse to make a new verse:
7. Change Ten to Nine.
8. Delete the words: Standing in a line
9. Delete the words: opened her mouth too far
10. Change nine to eight
    Now it should look like this:

        Ten little schoolchildren
        Standing in a line
        One opened her mouth too far
        And then there were nine.

        Nine little schoolchildren

        One
        And then there were eight.

11. Fill in the gaps to make a new verse
12. Remember the last word in the second line must rhyme with eight
13. Now do the same thing to make the next verse, and so on
    If you want to change schoolchildren to something else, such as dinosaurs or aliens, do so.
    Save your work often.

Improving Literacy with ICT © Trevor Millum 2012

Pupil worksheet B

Marking a text

Read the poem 'The Ballad of Unicorn Isle'.

There is print version and a version for your computer.

On the computer, you can any of these items to mark the text:

- Underline
- Bold
- Italic
- Coloured text
- Different fonts
- Different sizes of letter
- The highlighter pen

Use whichever you like in order to:

1. Pick out unusual or interesting words.
2. Find words which describe light or colour.
3. Find rhyming words and mark them so that rhymes can be clearly seen.
4. Pick out alliteration.

Here's an example, not using colour:

'I saw the future far **away** –
Hearken friends to what I **say**!
I saw **grey night** and I saw **grey day**
In the future far **away**!

Can you see how each feature of the poem has been marked in a different way?

An unusual word is shown by …
Alliteration is shown by …
Rhymes are show by ….
Reference to colour/light is shown by …

Now have a go at marking up the poem yourself.

The Ballad of Unicorn Isle

Once upon a faraway time
Before the clocks had learned to chime
When every river spoke in rhyme
Once upon a time

Once within a distant land
Where mountains hadn't heard of man
Where dolphins played and bluebirds sang
Once within a land

Then and there in echoing light
Where gold was day and silver night
Lived unicorns of purest black and white
There in echoing light

One shining day in shimmering shade
The seer had come to speak they said
An ancient one with eyes of jade
One shimmering shining day

'I saw the future far away –
Hearken friends to what I say!
I saw grey night and I saw grey day
In the future far away!

I saw the pale two-legged beast
Rise up from west, rise up from east
And slay our kind for fun and feast
The pale two-legged beast.

It hunted down the unicorn
It cut off head, it cut off horn
Or stole our foals as they were born
And caged the noble unicorn.'

Once upon a desperate hour
In the shadow of the great moonflower
They made a pact to use their power
Upon a desperate hour

So faded they from human sight
Though wild geese see them from their flight
And children dream of them at night
Invisible to human sight

Once within a faraway land
Where unicorns first heard of man
Where hotels rise and tourists tan
Once within a land…

© Trevor Millum

Improving Literacy with ICT © Trevor Millum 2012

Ways of marking a text

Extract from 'Jabberwocky' by Lewis Carroll:

Twas <u>brilli**g**</u>, and the <u>slithy</u> <mark>toves</mark>
Did **g**yre and **g**imble in the <mark>wabe</mark> :
All <u>mimsy</u> were the <mark>borogoves</mark> ,
And the <u>mome</u> <mark>raths</mark> outgrabe.

'*Beware the* Jabberwock, my son!
The jaws that bite, *the claws that* catch!
Beware the Jubjub bird, and shun
The <u>frumious</u> Bandersnatch!'

He took his <u>vorpal</u> sword in hand:
Long time the <u>manxome</u> foe he sought -
So res†ed he by the Tumtum tree,
And stood awhile in thought.

And, as in <u>uffish</u> thought he stood,
The Jabberwock, with eyes of flame,
Came WHIFFLING through the <u>tulgey</u> wood,
And BURBLED as it came!

Ways of marking the text

Bold	same sound (alliteration)
<u>Underline</u>	new adjectives
<mark>Grey highlight</mark>	new nouns
SMALL CAPS	new verbs describing sounds and movement
Italic	repetition
Marching black ants	interesting image

Digital teaching and learning in the primary classroom

The advent of ICT in all its forms has opened up enormous possibilities for teaching and learning in English. However, our underlying principles remain the same. We want to help young people develop their abilities in the wide range of human endeavour covered by the term 'communication', the crucial C of ICT. From expressing themselves clearly and creatively to understanding and appreciating what they hear, read and watch.

Rather than the four way division into Reading, Writing, Speaking and Listening, new technology has made it possible to see that there are really only two modes of communication: in and out. We create and express ourselves by speaking, by writing, by recording ourselves, even making films or having a computer translate our speech into text. In the other direction we receive communication from others by listening, reading and watching. We may 'read' a book by listening to a recording or 'chat' online by typing messages.

What remains the same is our need to develop all these processes in the interests of our pupils. Technology can be a help or a hindrance and we (and they) need to learn to use it when it is appropriate. In our teaching, we should use it when it can extend what we already do, make it more efficient or enable us to do things in ways which were previously not possible.

To take a few examples:

- we already encourage children to rework what they have written in order to improve it (and not, we hope, merely to correct spellings). ICT in the form of word processing, enables this to happen much more efficiently. We have always wanted pupils to look closely at texts.
- By hiding and revealing, de-sequencing or creating alphabetically 'collapsed' texts, we can achieve this in new and motivating ways.
- Class magazines have always been popular and teachers developed all sorts of ways of creating and 'publishing' them. ICT enables us to desktop publish and run off multiple copies (if the school photocopying budget allows) or, of course, publish on the school website.
- Digital voice recorders enable us to do things which were (in the majority of schools) impossible before. We can record children's voices away from a computer, download the recordings, *edit* them and play them back – all using inexpensive hardware and free software.

Together with all these opportunities come dangers, naturally, and we are not here talking about e-safety. The advent of the internet has made accessing information easy. It has not increased pupil's ability to sift and manage this information. Pupils used to copy chunks of information from reference books, now they can cut and paste them electronically. Summarising, note-taking, judging the quality of sources – all need to be taught and learnt.

Improving Literacy with ICT sets out to show how we can use the technology to achieve our goals. Along the way, you will think of other, new, ways of using it. In addition, you will have the confidence to know when a good book and the teacher's voice is all that is required – and cannot be improved upon.

To put a text into alphabetical order

(acknowledgements to Chris Warren)

Save the text first!

1.
Highlight text – and keep highlighted throughout

2.
Edit
Replace
Type a space in the top box
Type a ^p in the lower box
Replace All
(No)
Close

3.
Table
Sort
OK

4.
Edit
Replace
Type ^p in top box
Type a space or two or three in the lower box
Replace All
(No)
Close

Save with a new filename

Coded texts

Here are some coded texts to solve. Shorter texts might seem easier but you have fewer opportunities to spot repetitions. Be aware, too, of symbols which look similar but which are in fact different.

1. Nursery rhyme

🙰♋♍& ♋■♎ 🙰♓●● ⬥♏■⧫ ◆◻ ⧫♒♏ ♒♓●●
⧫□ ♐♏⧫♍♒ ♋ ◻♋♓● □♐ ⬥♋⧫♏❒
🙰♋♍& ♐♏●● ♎□⬥■ ♋■♎ ♌❒□&♏ ♒♓⬧ ♍❒□⬥■
♋■♎ 🙰♓●● ♍♋❍♏ ⧫◆❍♌●♓■♑ ♋♐⧫♏❒

2. Tongue twister (clue – it's about Betty Botter)

♌♏⧫⧫⍓ ♌□⧫⧫♏❒ ♌□◆♑♒⧫ ⬧□❍♏ ♌◆⧫⧫♏❒
♌◆⧫ ⬧♒♏ ⬧♋♓♎ ⧫♒♓⬧ ♌◆⧫⧫♏❒⬧ ♌♓⧫⧫♏❒
♌◆⧫ ♋ ♌♓⧫ □♐ ♌♏⧫⧫♏❒ ♌◆⧫⧫♏❒ ⬥♓●● ❍♋&♏ ❍⍓
♌◆⧫⧫♏❒ ♌♏⧫⧫♏❒
⬧□ ⬧♒♏ ♌□◆♑♒⧫ ⬧□❍♏ ♌♏⧫⧫♏❒ ♌◆⧫⧫♏❒
♌♏⧫⧫♏❒ ⧫♒♋■ ⧫♒♏ ♌♓⧫⧫♏❒ ♌◆⧫⧫♏❒
♋■♎ ♓⧫ ❍♋♎♏ ♒♏❒ ♌◆⧫⧫♏❒ ♌♏⧫⧫♏❒
⬧□ ♓⧫ ⬥♋⬧ ♌♏⧫⧫♏❒ ♌♏⧫⧫⍓ ♌□⧫⧫♏❒ ♌□◆♑♒⧫ ♋ ♌♓⧫
□♐ ♌♏⧫⧫♏❒ ♌◆⧫⧫♏❒

3. A coded story – the beginning of a traditional tale

□	■	♍	♏		◆	◻	□	■		♋		⧫	♓	❍	♏		●	□	■	♑		♋	♑	□		♋		&	♓	■	♑		♋	■	♎	
❑	◆	♏	♏	■		❒	◆	●	♏	♎		□	❖	♏	❒		♋		♎	♓	⬧	⧫	♋	■	⧫		●	♋	■	♎						
⧫	♒	♏		❑	◆	♏	♏	■		⬥	♋	⬧		&	♓	■	♎		♋	■	♎		♋	●	●		⧫	♒	♏		◻	♏	□	◻	●	♏
□	♐		⧫	♒	♏		❒	♏	♋	●	❍		♋	♎	□	❒	♏	♎		♒	♏	❒					⧫	♒	♏		□	■	●	⍓		
⬧	♋	♎	■	♏	⬧	⬧		♓	■		♒	♏	❒		●	♓	♐	♏		⬥	♋	⬧		⧫	♒	♋	⧫		⬧	♒	♏		♒	♋	♎	
■	□		♍	♒	♓	●	♎	❒	♏	■																										
□	■	♏		⬥	♓	■	⧫	♏	❒		♎	♋	⍓		⧫	♒	♏		❑	◆	♏	♏	■		⬥	♋	⬧		⬧	♏	⬥	♓	■	♑		
⬥	♒	♓	●	♏		●	□	□	&	♓	■	♑		□	◆	⧫		□	♐		⧫	♒	♏		⬥	♓	■	♎	□	⬥		♋	⧫			
⧫	♒	♏		⬧	■	□	⬥																													
♋		♌	♓	❒	♎		♐	●	♏	⬥		♌	⍓		⧫	♒	♏		⬥	♓	■	♎	□	⬥		⬧	⧫	♋	❒	⧫	●	♓	■	♑		
⧫	♒	♏		❑	◆	♏	♏	■		♋	■	♎		⬧	♒	♏		◻	❒	♓	♍	&	♏	♎		♒	♏	❒		♐	♓	■	♑	♏	❒	
♋		⬧	♓	■	♑	●	♏		♎	❒	□	◻		□	♐		♌	●	□	□	♎		♐	♏	●	●		□	■		⧫	♒	♏			
⬧	■	□	⬥		□	◆	⧫	⬧	♓	♎	♏		♒	♏	❒		⬥	♓	■	♎	□	⬥														
⬧	♒	♏		⬧	♋	♓	♎		⧫	□		♒	♏	❒	⬧	♏	●	♐		♓		⬥	♓	⬧	♒		♓		♒	♋	♎		♋			
♎	♋	◆	♑	♒	⧫	♏	❒		⬥	♓	⧫	♒		⬧	&	♓	■		♋	⬧		⬥	♒	♓	⧫	♏		♋	⬧		⬧	■	□	⬥		
●	♓	◻	⬧		♋	⬧		❒	♏	♎		♋	⬧		♌	●	□	□	♎		♋	■	♎		♒	♋	♓	❒		♋	⬧					
♌	●	♋	♍	&		♋	⬧		♍	□	♋	●																								

Website response form

Website:

	Very	Quite	OK	Not very	Not at all
How easy is it to understand?					
How useful for your purpose?					
How reliable do you think it is?					
How easy is it to find what you need?					
Other comments					

Website response form

Website:

	Very	Quite	OK	Not very	Not at all
How easy is it to understand?					
How useful for your purpose?					
How reliable do you think it is?					
How easy is it to find what you need?					
Other comments					

A glossary of common ICT terms

blinds: a feature of software which accompanies most interactive whiteboards, allowing 'blinds' to be drawn from the top, bottom or sides of the screen in order to hide parts of the display.

blog: an online journal or diary that allows users to publish material instantly using tools that allow the incorporation of multimedia resources as well as text. Blogger, Typepad and WordPress are examples of popular blogging services.

browser: the software program that displays web pages, such as Mozilla Firefox, Internet Explorer and Safari.

cropping tool: a tool used in the editing of images, allowing the user to make a smaller image by cropping the top, bottom or sides of a picture.

data projector : a device enabling the display on a computer to be projected onto a wall or screen. It does not require an interactive whiteboard but is often used in conjunction with one.

dialogue box: a window which opens while you are using a program, requesting some input from the user. For example, when Ctrl P is pressed, a 'print' dialogue box opens.

digital camera: a camera that records images in digital format rather than on film; many allow video recording as well as still photography

digital projector: another term for data projector (qv)

find and replace: a function of word processors which allows the user to search for a word or phrase and replace it with something different. It can also be used to find and replace a wide range of features such as fonts, highlighting and punctuation.

Google Docs: a web-based word processor, spreadsheet, presentation, form and data storage service offered by Google. This free Web 2.0 service allows users to create and edit documents online, collaborating in real-time with other users; see: docs.google.com.

highlight: a tool available in many word processors, enabling text to be emphasized by the use of a digital pen which leaves a mark similar to a coloured highlighter pen.

hyperlink: an area (text or an image) in a document such as a web page which links to another location, either another part of the document or to another document such as a website. Normally clicking on a hyperlink with a mouse takes the user to the new location. Text hyperlinks are usually underlined to identify them, though other conventions such as a contrasting colour are sometimes used.

ICT: information and communication technology: used to indicate the specifically educational applications of technology.

insert comment: a feature of some word processors which enables the user to attach a comment to a specific part of the text. The comment is usually displayed in the margin.

interactive whiteboard: a large interactive display connected to a computer and digital projector. Users can control the display from the computer using a pen, finger or other device on the board.

intranet: a network set up by an organization such as a school for internal use – in other words, unlike the internet, this is normally private.

learning platform: an integrated system to provide information, tools and resources for education, including teaching and learning materials, recording and assessment systems, messaging, wikis, blogs, etc. Also known as a virtual learning environment (VLE) or managed learning environment (MLE), it is usually delivered through a web interface and accessible from both inside and outside the institution. Moodle is an open source example; there are numerous commercial services.

macro: a feature of software programs such as word processors which allow the user to 'record' a series of key presses or mouse clicks. This can be saved so that you can quickly repeat the same process by using a keyboard shortcut.

multimodal/multimodality: a combination of modes of communication, for example, combining graphics, text and audio output with speech, text and touch input.

offline: working with computers while unconnected to the internet. An offline application does not rely on a connection for it to work.

PDF: portable document format, devised by the Adobe Corporation to allow the creator to share a document with its design fixed. Others can read and print PDF documents but can only edit them with special software. Adobe provides free software, sometimes called the Acrobat reader, which enables users to open PDF documents automatically.

podcast: a portmanteau word combining 'broadcast' and 'iPod' and originally meaning a file (usually audio, sometimes video) stored on a website and then broadcast using a web feed; now used more loosely to describe an audio file found on a website.

right-click: a PC mouse has two buttons – left and right; performing a right-click often brings up an alternative set of choices or a menu.

sort function: a feature of word processors, allowing words or lines to be sorted into alphabetical order.

spotlight: a feature of software which accompanies most interactive whiteboards. Most of the screen is invisible but a movable 'window' of light enables viewers to see and focus on a small area of the whiteboard display.

URL: uniform resource locator – the address used by web browsers to locate a resource on the internet, such as http://www.nate.org.uk.

USB: universal serial bus, a standard for communication between a computer and external devices using a cable; most modern computers have several USB ports that permit the connection of printers, cameras, scanners, USB memory drives ('flash drives', 'pen drives' or 'thumb drives'), etc.

visualizer: a piece of equipment which projects an image from, say, the teacher's desk onto a screen via a data projector. It can be used to show, for example, pupils' work, pictures or text from books or 3D objects. Most will also have a facility to save images.

VLE: virtual learning environment: another term used to describe a learning platform (qv)

Web 2.0: the generic term for web applications that enable interactive information sharing and collaboration on the World Wide Web. Examples include social networking sites, blogs and wikis, emphasizing peer-to-peer relationships rather than the top-down ones found on static web pages.

wiki: a website that can be edited by users; Wikipedia and Wikispaces are examples.

Further reading and browsing

Websites

National Association for the Teaching of English: NATE is the UK subject teacher association for all aspects of English from preschool to university level. There is an area on the NATE site devoted to English and ICT: www.nate.org.uk/ict

Teachit: an online repository of resources, many free, and interactive materials for subscribers: www.teachit.co.uk. You might like to sign up for the very useful compendium of ideas and techniques delivered once a week for a year – the Teachit Tips service, recommended if you enjoy exploring magic tricks on a computer! http://bit.ly/te_27

The British Library: access to some of the unrivalled resources of one of the world's great libraries. See especially *Turning the Pages* and the *Learning* section for resources on both language and literature: www.bl.uk

Books

While these texts are aimed mainly at English teaching in a secondary setting, they contain ideas and approaches that may well be of interest.

NATE ICT Committee, edited by Trevor Millum and Chris Warren: *Sharing, Not Staring*, NATE 2008; seventeen interactive whiteboard lessons for the English classroom, with CD.

Trevor Millum and Chris Warren: *Twenty Things to do with a Word Processor*, Resource (also available from NATE), second edition 2005: photocopiable pages with easy-to-use ideas throughout the secondary age range.

Tony Archdeacon: *Exciting ICT in English*, Network Educational Press, 2005

Andrew Goodwyn (ed.): *English in the Digital Age*; information and communications technology and the teaching of English, Cassell, 2000

Moira Monteith (ed.): *Teaching Secondary School Literacies with ICT*, Open University Press, 2005

Index

Descriptors such as writing, reading, speaking and listening have not been included in the index, for obvious reasons. Neither have word processors or software applications such as Word or PowerPoint. A key term omitted from the index is *creativity*, which comprises a continuous thread throughout the book and, if indexed, would appear on every page.